VOYAGES

By the same author

Poems
Fishermen with Ploughs
Loaves and Fishes
The Year of the Whale
Winterfold
Selected Poems

Short Stories
A Calendar of Love
A Time to Keep
Hawkfall
The Sun's Net
Andrina

Play
A Spell for Green Corn

Novels
Greenvoe
Magnus

Essays
An Orkney Tapestry
(Gollancz)
Letters from Hamnavoe
(Gordon Wright Publishing)
Under Brinkie's Brae
(Gordon Wright Publishing)

Non-Fiction
Portrait of Orkney
(with photographs by Werner Forman)

For Children
The Two Fiddlers
Pictures in the Cave
Six Lives of Fankle the Cat

VOYAGES

George Mackay Brown

CHATTO & WINDUS

THE HOGARTH PRESS

LONDON

Published in 1983 by
Chatto & Windus · The Hogarth Press
40 William IV Street
London WC2N 4DF

All rights reserved. No part of this
publication may be reproduced, stored in
a retrieval system or transmitted in any
form, or by any means, electronic, mechanical,
photocopying, recording or otherwise, without
the prior permission of the publisher.

British Library Cataloguing in Publication Data

Brown, George Mackay
   Voyages.
   I. Title
   821'.914   PR6052.R/
ISBN 0-7011-2736-8

© George Mackay Brown 1983

Printed in Great Britain by
Redwood Burn Ltd
Trowbridge, Wiltshire

To Nora

Contents

SEAL ISLAND ANTHOLOGY
Market Day   9
Minister   9
Fishing Boats in a Fog   9
Widower   9
Croft Wife   10
Dead Faces   10
Rain   10
Blacksmith   10
Letter   11
Wisdom   11
American   11
Gossip about a Girl   11
Nocturne   12
Pig Sticker   12
Snow   12
Ploughing Match   12
Clock   13
Scarecrow   13
Envy   13
Cat   13
The Laird's Garden   14
Gravestone   14
Aurora   15
Snow and Thaw   15
Mulled Ale   16
Lessons   16
Wanderer   16

*

Bird in the Lighted Hall   19
Magi   20
Letters to the River   22
Hamnavoe Market   26
Voyager   27
Sally: A Pastoral   29
A Christmas Patchwork   31
Vinland   34

Lighting Candles in Midwinter 36
The Star to Every Wandering Barque 37
A Joyful Mystery 38
Orkneymen at Clontarf 40
William and Mareon Clark 43
Countryman 48

SEAL ISLAND ANTHOLOGY

Market Day
    He came back from the town
    With news
    Of fighting in Russia
    And red things like tatties (apples)
    And sixpenny spectacles —
    His eyes were big as an ox.

Minister
    Polish twelve boots.
    Run
    To the well for water
    To splash faces in:
    Kirstag has seen
    The boat rowing from Rousay,
    A black column in it.

Fishing Boats in Fog
    Rob's boat is in, blinded,
    A thin catch.
    The *Teeack* had nothing. (Mist, sun-pearl.)
    Rob, did you see Tam and Mansie?
    What ghost is this
    Driven by insane pewter swirls?

Widower
    Old Stephen three winters now
    Has spoken to none
    But his cat
    And the spider at the back of his bed
    And himself
    And to a stone in the kirkyard
    With thirteen names
    (The last cut sharp and deep).

Croft Wife
  Make ale. Make
  Butter, cheese, bread (small suns).
  Make
  Every summer the nine-fold rounding
  Moon shape.
  Make fire. Make a star
  In the frozen well.

Dead Faces
  When I saw that first star-coldness
  I was a child.
  I have seen faces the sea had eaten
  And pain-clenched faces
  And faces like flowers, gathered.
  I have seen the face of a dead man
  Who still
  Laughs, bargains, boasts.

Rain
  A gray hoof whirled at the sun, splinterings
  Of blue and yellow and orange.
  I felt
  Corn cells, underfoot, gorging.
  A trout
  Flashed from the salt into brief sweetness.

Blacksmith
  As the wild bees
  Forge
  Sweetness under a stone
  As roots in darkness
  Hammer up
  Clusters of the may-flower

  Since the lass of Clett
  Was here
  With her father's plough to patch
  I go with sun pieces
  Between forge and wincing anvil.

Letter
    Dear parents, at last
        You hear from me.
            The day
        I went to Kirkwall for feeing
            A kind-spoken sailor
    Asked me to broach a bottle in his cabin.
        I woke among wastes of sea.
I am well. I write this
        At a table of black gold-ringed hands.

Wisdom
    Say, 'I have seen the migrant sail dwindling west.'
    Say, 'Golden hand among fallen stalks.'
    Say, 'We ate seaweed and limpets one spring.'
    Say, 'I have closed ten eyes, or a dozen eyes.'
    Say, 'The laird gets younger and greedier.'
    Say, 'They increase, the things beyond utterance.'
    Then it's time
    To leave dark lamp and folded breath
    And row old into the dayspring.

American
    Sander is home again
    Twanging
    Music from the root of his nose.

Gossip about a Girl
    'She goes like the burdened bee'....
    'The slut. The shame'....
    'She has the face of a bairn that keeps a bird in
                    the cage of her hands'....
    'The moon wheel turns. The ninth round knits
               with the wheel of the
                sun, as burn is meshed
                into ocean'....
    'She goes, in secret, migrant to cranny'....
    'That my hidden silver (it rots) might be hers'....

Nocturne
    The candle draught-flung. I hit
    The shadow
    At the pane with my pillow.
    I hit it with nails and feet.
    I hit the stranger
    (That smelt like Willie of Gorse)
    Again and again
    With the rose of my mouth.

Pig Sticker
    The sweet pigling
    Squandered
    His life in shower on shower of roses.

    The bairns
    Put drained faces against the wall.

    He washed, later
    In gray water, the single beast-petal off.

Snow
    The young men went
            Here and there, secret
        At star-time.
           Black swirls — a sudden
    Blanket of snow!
           And the blank
                At dawn, a maze
                    Of silvery tell-tale trystings.

Ploughing Match
    If you come tonight
    Fisherman
    Take the track from the shore.
    The hill road
    Is reeling with malt-red ploughboys.

Clock
    We had the sun, stars, shadow.
    Today
    In Greta's house, a box
    Of numbers and wheels
    And cleek-cleek, click-clock, that insect
    Eating time at the wall.

Scarecrow
    A stick and tatter
    I lean into the sun's loom.

Envy
    I wish I was Andrew
    Standing
    With a bright shivering ring
    Beside that tall whiteness
    In the hushed barn
    Tonight
    When the minister urges the gold circlet from fingers to finger.

    I would rather be Andrew
    Than the laird
    With a sideboard of silver plate
    And silk hangings
    And his seat in the parliament.

    I would rather be
    That ploughman
    Than General Wellington on his stone snorting horse
    Or George our king stamped on a thousand coins.

Cat (to Dave Brock)
    Swingler came in soft slippers.
    My trout was needles
    Before the knife could flash at the silver belly.

    Swingler, pirate, with one patched eye
    Unlocked
    My golden cube of butter.

Swingler, exile, sits at my fire
　　All the six nights
　　The moon locks herself in her crystal cave.

　　My peats rage red on the winter stone.
　　Swingler sings.

The Laird's Garden
　　Idle summer out (said the bee)
　　There are no jars
　　In a cupboard of the House of Winter
　　For drifters and dandlers and dreamers.

　　Plunder the sun (said the butterfly)
　　Smoulder. Save. Scheme.
　　Mask-and-Glove take all, at last.

　　See the gowned ladies and tulips going (said the bee)
　　See, in the kirkyard,
　　A swirl of scented dust.

　　The queen of the lucent combs (said the butterfly)
　　Where is she
　　When the Ice King
　　Walks through the garden in his ancient armour?

Gravestone
　　Suddenly a stone chirped
　　Bella's goodness,
　　Faithfulness,
　　Fruitfulness,
　　The numbers
　　Of Bella's beginning and end.
　　It sang like a harp, the stone!

　　James-William
　　Put a shilling
　　In the dusty palm of the carver.

　　Wind, snow, sun grainings.

Sixth door, seventh door, eighth door
Barred.
I stood, a cancelled man, in the rain.

Twilight in the ninth door,
A star, a kiss.

When I come to the last door,
Take me, earth,
From eight earth-gold and sea-silvered hands.

Perhaps I will think of you eating alone.
The little white cat
Has already devoured the eyes and the tail.

My fingers stink. I will dip them in scented water.
I will put a flower in a cup
As soon as the first star is out. Then
Men will carry me on poles to the theatre.

    4
Is this not good news?

A man came up-river in a skiff.
I stood among the reeds.
He said, 'I will tell what I have seen.'
He pushed with his oar into midstream
Going urgently down-river, then.

I wondered, between two moons
About the boatman and his words.
Now I have a letter.
A horseman brought it on a stick.

The lord is to come upstream
Next week, in a barge.

'Talk of your comeliness has made me young again.'

    5
I have written many letters to you.
The old man
Takes back no letter from your hand.

The old man says, 'The second letter
Did not make him weep
But there were old tear-stains on his face.
The fourth letter, perhaps the fifth
Made him laugh.
(Not river laughter, more like a masker.)

Your last letter
He put behind the nets, unread.

Once he gave me a cup of wine.
He said, *Drink, man*
To a river girl of two summers ago.'

   6
I am leaving this house soon.
I will live in a villa.
The garden is a mile outside the city.
I am to have two servants.
A boy gets silver to go errands.
You will not be seeing the old man any more.
The old man
Is ashes in a pot, a quiet ghost in the garden,
                                      wandering.

I am learning to ride a horse.
Bathing me, combing my hair, dressing me
The two women call me 'lady'.
I can pour wine now without spilling a drop,
I can write a dozen words on silk.
I am forgetting the river language.

Perhaps my horse will stop near the jetties.
I always look at the boats
As I pass on my way to the city.

   7
It was told me, 'A fisherman
Was taken two days ago from the river.'

My heart was a hive of questions.
Did the nets entangle you?
Perhaps there is water in your lungs.
Will your sister come?
Will your sister nurse you among the nets?

compared to the comely nakedness of the savages. This is what the gold seekers have come to, penury and sickness.

December 15: We saw Balth this day, talking with some brown men in a village. Their faces opened with white flashes. They chewed sticks. Balth gathered us into the company. *We are near the place*, he said. *The old map was useless. I have spoken with the Indians.* A black boy marked the dust with a star. Balth gave cuts of tobacco to the village men. *I knew we would come together here*, he said. *Perhaps tomorrow night, perhaps the night after. It is worth the broken feet, a small betrayal.*

Letters to the River

1
I am expecting a caller tonight.
Do not take river smells to my door.

I send this scroll by an old man.
He does this and that for a small coin.
He cannot read.
Do not say a harsh word to the old man.

The old man's daughter stitches my masks.
Either she has put a flower in the window
Or a gray unlit candle.
(The cold wax for nights I do not dance)

2
I have never been better off.
I have three coats, large butterflies, across the bed.
I have a purse with a silk cord.
Gifts are left at my door.
A poet I have never seen
Is, they say, praising me in the villages.
And the children imitate my dances.

3
I see a horseman coming between the gardens.
I wonder how things are with you?
Are you catching a fish or two off the island?
A river fish has been left at my door.
Did you come by last night?
If so, I thank you. Gifts come like autumn leafage
                                        in the doorway.

I cut the fish into fine pieces.
The slices are drying in the wind.
I will set them on a plate tonight, for my guest,
In a circle of blossoms.

The stone's a whisper now.
Soon
The stone will be silence.

Aurora
The Arctic girl is out tonight.
(Come to the doors.)
She dances
In a coat of yellow and green patches.
She bends
Over the gate of the stars.

What is she, a tinker lass?
Does she carry flashing cans
From the quarry fires?

I think
She's a princess in a silk gown.
She holds
A bowl of green cut crystal.

Come to the doors!
She is walking about in the north, the winter witch.

Snow and Thaw
The first snowflake we called
"silver moth".

We hailed the hill next morning —
Moby Dick!

Sun on sea,
blue silver blinding
mirrors.

The thaw, it was like an old filthy tramp
that had slept
in a ditch in the rain.

Mulled Ale
    The circus in Hamnavoe,
        Is that a fact,
            A man swallowing fire,
    A clown with patched cheeks?
        You should see Jock
      After he's stuck the red-hot poker
Five or six times in the ale pot.

Lessons
    Chants the young schoolmaster
        'First arithmetic. . . .
        'Now spelling. . . .
        'Now dates, kings and battles. . . .'
A butterfly loiters past the pane.
      Sam has a burning punished hand
Because of a wind-flung flower and a cloud.

        'Now geography. . . .'
Book-bent heads. The first Arctic bird
Crosses the window between ice and roses.

Wanderer
    I stood at ten doors in that island.

In the first door
I was shown the tooth of the dog.

In the second door
A stinking fish was put in my hand.

Senseless unprofitable babblings
In the third door.

A fiddle like a tortured cat
In the fourth door.

In the fifth door
A skull wrapped in a shawl, whisperings.

Bird in the Lighted Hall

The old poet to his lute:
'Bright door, black door,
Beak-and-wing hurtling through,
This is life.
(Childhood lucent as dew,
The opening rose of love,
Labour at plough and oar,
The yellow leaf,
The last blank of snow.)
Hail and farewell. Too soon
The song is mute,
The spirit free and flown.
But you, ivory bird, cry on and on
To guest and ghost
From the first stone
To the sag and fall of the roof.'

Magi (to Katia and Dominique)

June 24: This day Karlson, Balth and I left the ship *Thor* secretly, and rowed in a small boat to one of a hundred islands. Sand burned, sun poured unbearable gold upon us.

June 27: The map was plain in the mind of Balth. He drew it with his toe in the sand, and put an X where was the treasure. We have been to two islands. There is no word of the place.

July 1: Black and brown faces flee from our guns. But the forest is full of eyes. The water low in the skins. The night flies have bored me, arm and thigh.

August 18: How long we have lain in this village, in a hut, I do not know. The fever has branded us, all three. The ruined eyes of an old black man watched our shivering bones. Insects and honey he put in our mouths.

August 20: Karlson was first on his feet. He staggered like a drunk man. The old man laughed.

September 29: Balth has left us, two days ago. Balth has taken the map that was in his mind. *They are a burden to me.* Did Balth say that? Yet he was a good companion. May he find the silver, may it sweeten his age. We are free and lost, Karlson and I.

October 8: With Karlson and me, the only desire is to find a port with ships. Black hands point. *There, there the sails, beyond two rivers and a forest. . . .*

November 21: One night lately was full of shapes of terror. Sleeping then, after the sun made branches black upon red, I dreamed I was a child in Orkney, and I owned the whole world, cow and buttercup and rockpool, and the men and women and animals put looks of love on me and on each other.

Then to awake to the scarred face of Karlson, and mosquitoes, and smoke of a volcano, and a hidden screaming parrot.

December 1: The nights have been cold. Even the smaller heights wear snow capes. In the port, one Spanish ship. A poster on the harbour-master's door: concerning absconded sailors, a reward, 3 familiar names. We drank the harbour-master's rum.

December 8: We have nothing. We have no skill to catch wild creatures for the fire. The few rags on us are shameful

Perhaps he is dead.
He has gone perhaps with blue hands and a crab-eaten
face into the fire.

Now, at last, a letter. 'I thank you.
I only suffered a cold in the throat.
No, I will not come
To live with the butterflies in your garden.
I am uncaring and cold
Whoever enters your fine door or leaves it.'

Why do I still think in the evenings
Of the river and the river smell and river words?

Hamnavoe Market

No school today! We drove in our gig to the town.
Daddo bought us each a coloured balloon.
Mine was yellow, it hung high as the moon.
A cheapjack urged. Swingboats went up and down.

Coconuts, ice-cream, apples, ginger beer
Routed the five bright shillings in my pocket.
I won a bird-on-a-stick and a diamond locket.
The Blind Fiddler, the broken-nosed boxers were there.

The booths huddled like mushrooms along the pier.
I ogled a goldfish in its crystal cell.
Round every reeling corner came a drunk.

The sun whirled a golden hoof. It lingered. It fell
On a nest of flares. I yawned. Old Madge our mare
Homed through a night black as a bottle of ink.

Voyager
(to Dennis O'Driscoll)

On the third morning
We came to the whale acre.
No whales, the net
Surged with a galaxy of herring.
The raven, uncaged,
Fluttered over hidden islands.

On the eighth morning
A buttercup braid
Came down to meet us at a shore.
Her name was Gudrun.
A bluebell eye
Led us to hall and husband,
Harp, alehorn, fine flowers of flame.

No man, flame-fettered, finds fame
Or lockfast gold.
On the twentieth morning
We dared the dark whirls,
Furious looms of sea.
There *Hawkwing* left us,
Whether
Broken in the salt shuttles
Or set on private pillage westward
We have not known.

We had small luck
With the holy crosses, the halls
Of Gaelic chiefs.
All were empty, all
Bore the famous brand marks.
Our fathers
Had been that way before.
Our fathers have left
Fine stories, burnt stones.
We sat hungry
Between a loch and a mountain

On the hundredth morning, under
The fourth moon.

Ragna, I write this
From an Irish village.
Are you still in the world,
I wonder
With your loom and querns and cheese-mould?
I am a gray humped man.
I had to learn new speech long ago.
I tend horses in a field.
After ten thousand mornings
Of rain, frost, larksong
How should I find a way back
To the waterfront of Trondheim?

Sally : A Pastoral
(to Charles Cansley)

   1
Three harvest days she wasn't at school.
Sally was ill!
Now
I hear from the stooks a summons, a challenge, a call.
There's the brighter sweep of her brow
Among the broken gold of the hill!

   2
'Sally,
You'll be in trouble, you're late for school.'
She listened, loitered, lingered.
Silent, she ebbed and eddied and flowed.
She fingered
Gray blobs of wool
From a twang and reverberation of barbed wire,
The truant, Sally.
Larks rained round her, out of a cloud
An unlearned shower.

   3
Sally and I fought.
I got
An eye like a plum.
I have from her
Three strands of sunbright hair
Between my bleeding fingers and thumb.

   4
From the top of the Ward
A turning head can see
The ring of the whole earth, with the western
                              sunset smoulder.
Hallward he rides, the laird.
In the heather, the first stirrings of midge and moth.
The yawls, with their shifting silver, are in
                              from the sea.

(I have laid three fish at her door.)
Now the west is a jet and crimson bar.
The wind blows colder.
There's none under the first star
But Sally and me.
Earth wrecks on a reef of stars, and drowns us both.

   5
Sally, bride
Glides like a swan
Into the psalming kirk.
The wedding guests have all gone in.
I turn, alone, outside
As the ox plods to its winter work.

A Christmas Patchwork

Inn Keeper
    I know you, Tomas the shepherd-boy.
    A skin of wine, is it?
    Tell them, no skins of wine for hillmen.
    Take that cold face
    Up among the cold stars.
    Tell them, a new lamb
    Might broach a barrel.
    The rabble again —
    Taxmen, yokels, tarts, soldiers.
      *
    Not another knock!

Census Official
    Names and occupations in order.
        Isaac, tribe of David, fisherman
        Saul, tribe of David, goat-herd
        Joshua, tribe of David, baker
            (It's Caesar Augustus
            Wants your names, not me.
            Soon as I see
            The last of your mules and drums,
            It's the bright lights for me, pronto.
            Make your star on the parchment.)
        Jacob, lineage of David, brick-maker.

Soldier
    No Miriam. I'm a soldier. It's midnight. I must go.
    The colonel said
    Sharpen your swords. I want
    An eye cold as a star
    Before the wakening of birds and children.

First King
>Fix on one star, at last,
>Any star
>In the circling star blizzard.
>That star will take you
>Whithersoever
>To Death and Birth and Love.

Herod
>Tramps, dogs, children with palms, recognize Herod
>The skull with the sun-crown.
>Kings would know a king, if the king
>Wore a leper cloth.
>I gaze, blind, through a golden mask.
>Look for star-troubled strangers.
>Under the merchant masks
>They are kings and king-seekers.
>Bring me word
>Where the masquers unload their bales.

Bedtime Story, Bethlehem
>There was this old Chinaman
>(Once on a star time)
>That king was yellow as a goldfish.
>He lived in a crystal palace.
>And one day came knocking on his door
>An Ebony king.
>And next noon came knocking
>An Ivory king.
>The three kings kissed. They crossed.
>They saddled mules. Their faces flushed with sunset.
>And then —
>*Wheest, the bairn's asleep.*

Second King
    A lantern at the gate, red as an apple.
    A village, clay houses.
    A lamp in every niche.
    We went on slowly, seeking
    The inn.
    (Sweet the wine bowl, bread, bason of water
    After such brandings of sun and sand.)
    At the inn
    One candleflame in a bottle, athwart
    A tumult of flushed mouths.
    In our chamber
    A star like a nail was the only light.

Priest
    Folded it is now, the dove,
    Furled, star-folded.
    The black rain falls, the bitter floods rise still.
    What hand
    Will take the branch from the dove's beak?

Third King
    We stand, three vagrants, at the last door.
    A black fist
    Lingers, a star, on withered wood.

Shepherd
    'No wine.' He wouldn't part with a skin or a bottle.
    It was closing time.
    'Come tomorrow,' the porter said.
    ('Bring a lamb,' said he.)
    'The inn-keeper's out of his wits
    With stars, soldiers, taxmen, foreigners, hill folk.'

Vinland

1
Wet shirt, breeches, kamiks
For a week
And a loud cough.
No blink of fire still
On the bleak
Unbroken circles of sea,
No singing throats
Between ship and shore.

2
The hungry raven
Astir in the basket. This
Is good, the bird
Eager
To be twelve masts up, turning!
That black hunger
Is smelling
Seeds and worms in the west.

3
Salt in the mouth,
The rage
Of north wind at morning,
Sodden crust,
Cold kissings of rain.
This unease
Is better than my Ragna at the hearth.

4
This heals heart,
On a blank stone westwards to cut
Such runes —
ICELANDERS
IN THE SUN'S LAST HOUSE
THE WILD GRAPES
STEEPED AND BODE NOT
BARRELS' BROACHING.

5
Too late for rudder's turning
Back into history,
The old worn web,
King, lawman, merchant, serf.
The prow crashes
Into a new time.

6
He that can cup in the ear
Spidersong, dewfall
(Six weeks I hear only
Salt monotony)
Has heard, ahead,
Sea fingers fringing shore foam.

7
They will say next winter
At the fires
'Leif Ericson went
The fool's voyage.'
A man will sing to a harp
'Heroes
Venture for more than bits of gold.'
An old woman will say
To girls at candle time
'It is that slut, the sea
Always
That has their hearts.'

Lighting Candles in Midwinter

Saint Lucy, see
Seven bright leaves in the winter tree

Seven diamonds shine
In the deepest darkest mine

Seven fish go, a glimmering shoal
Under the ice of the North Pole

Sweet St Lucy, be kind
To us poor and wretched and blind.

The Star to Every Wandering Barque
(for a 25th Wedding Anniversary)

Wave above wave — westward that night
The sea was a broken stair

In a house of menace, and never beacon or bell
To tell us where we were —

Near the great whirls, or close
To crag or reef or shallow (God knows where).

Above, thick-woven cloud. Beneath
The skull-strewn dragon lair.

How long, how late, since the ship
Had cleared the harbour bar

We made no reckoning soon. Our skipper plied
Ship-wit, sea-care.

(Will the heart keep tryst?
Does the dove, branch-burdened, quest through the
                                  perilous air?)

Precious the cargo,
Urgent the hunger that drew it from shore to shore.

Deep in the hold
The jars of love we bore.

All who trade in that freightage
Dread the devourings of time, and salt, and tare.

How could we have doubted?
Like a lantern in a barn door,

Like the roof-furled familiar dove,
Upon our voyage hung the homing star.

A Joyful Mystery
(Stations of the Cross)

He had left the tree, the ass, the apple basket.

We turned our faces back to the town.
One man had seen a boy traded for silver,
Gone on with camels then.

A boy had stood at a stone with bruised knees.

Boy after boy, blithe lissom corn-high faces,
Never the lonely sun-look.

We got to Simon's yard at noon.
He had lingered there.
On had danced, playing shepherds, reeds at his mouth.

At Veronica's he had asked for a basin.
She showed us the towel,
A splotch of happy dust and blood at the centre.

Three beggars sat with locked tongues
In the next village.
A stick wrote in the dust.

Women at the bleach-green stretched fingers.
An hour since, city-bound
Young hair indeed had streamed past.

We circled, slowly, a foot-print in dew.

A cloud,
Red tatters, the drained heart of the day.

Star scatter (grains of dead salt.) I laid
Skull beside breathing skull.

We took our skulls at dawn to the Dove Gate.
The market a tumult of ghosts and skulls.

Skulls traded, mimed, looked out of windows, smiled.
Ghosts came and flickered and went.

We drew, hollow-eyed, at noon, to the temple.
Doctors of law read tombstones
Under burst and burst of apple blossom.

Orkneymen at Clontarf

What are you doing here, Finn?
(I ask myself that.)
Today, Good Friday, the ox in Stronsay
Tears sweet grass
Beside an idle plough, the men
Go between kirk and smithy.
Panis angelicus sing
The priest and the boys.
   *

Sigurd is the name of our earl.
His mother the witch
Wove our black banner.
That raven croaks above the host.
Whoever bears the bird of victory
Drinks tonight in dark halls.
Now Sigurd alone
Offers the raven to a sackcloth sun.
   *

'If you go to Ireland,' she said
'Speak to the holy men
With their prayers and candles,
Not to the little kings
Offering bits of battle silver.'
That's what my mother said, in Westray.
I'm young. What do I want with a psalter?
The silver pieces
Will buy an ox for next ploughtime.
   *

What can be done with an arrow
Thrust
Deep in the rib-cage?
Paul, my friend, broke the shaft,
The barb shrieks inside still.
I am tired of this guest.
What's to be done with a hawk,
Hoverer, hungerer, heart-eater

Locked in the ribs?
The hand of a death-maiden keeps the key.
   *
I forget the name of the saint
That saved my grandfather
Under a burning wall of Paris one summer.
Whatever your name, white one
I am grandson
To old Olaf, that you kept from torrents
                           of lead and tar
That day in the Seine.
I intend to light a candle for you.
   *
I bought the horse in Dublin.
Seven times
It reared against horn and shield-wall.
Now it is hide and bone, that horse,
And tatters of blood
I am walking back to the town.
At the river mouth
The proud Minch-trampler is moored.
   *
'Now,' I said to the Hamnavoe girls
'I don't hunt crabs any more,
I'm a soldier of Sigurd.'
The girls fingered axe and creel.
Be still a fisherman, Nord.
A thousand fools get gathered
Into the net of battle.
It's the wolf, no silver gull-circle
Unravels the guts of warmen.
   *
Coming to Ireland
We stopped first at Barra.
A cold week, snow in the ale.
Coming to Ireland
About some royal mix-up or other
We stopped at Man.
I devoted an April day to bright edges.
Coming to Ireland

We have stopped at a noisy fair-ground, Clontarf.
The revellers
Wear red masks and patches.
 *
When they said, *Rolf is dead*
Under a hoof
I said, 'Fare on, Rolf.
It goes well with you, friend.
Flesh-unfastened,
A swift swallowflight soon
To the Hall of Heroes.'
Then I turned and gave release
To three Irish axemen.
 *
We drank thick ale in Galloway.
Brave boasting there —
Battles, blood, wall-breaching.
Now the glory is come
There is no ditch anywhere
I would not creep into,
Sharing a mushroom with tramp and slut.
 *
Sven said he would never
Come into Ireland.
'A place of enchantment, Ireland.'
Yet he sang with us at the rowing-bench
Down the broken coastline of Scotland.
Here
A white star has broken on Sven's brow.
 *
In Rousay this sunset
Under Scabra
Men will be lifting lobsters.
A girl at a rockpool
Is shaking out yellow hair.
If I do not get back from this battle
Tell the brewer at Kierfea
We have found a quieter alehouse,
Free drink, no hangovers.

William and Mareon Clark

1
The Opening of the Tavern: 1596

Johnsmas. The noon light clear and hard,
  He bade Mareon, his ship-shape wife
    Unlatch the new oak door.
No lingering man or beast in the yard.
    Not a foot crossed the sanded floor
  To chair and flagon, platter and knife.
      A barrel seethed in one corner, the best March ale.
    Five hams hung, cured in winter smoke.
From the kitchen, a fragrance and crispness of bread.
Beyond, clean bolsters and blankets spread.
     A house of keeping it was for far-come folk,
  With turf and driftwood to feed the welcoming flame.
Four days of silence. Nobody came.
  Then William said, 'Goodwife, I see
     Bad counsel I had from lawyer and shipman and earl
      Anent the lease of this inn
Here on a barren spit of shore.
    We will flourish here like the winter whin.
It's road and tinker rags for you and me'. . .

The next day (sea lash, gull whirl, gale)
    They saw a Frenchman anchor and furl
  From the outer Atlantic roar.
William and Mareon endured an anxious silence.
   Knockings and strange shouts soon at the gale-fast door.
    A brig blunders bayward, anchors and furls
Behind the two sheep islands.
Mareon's hand brims over with bread and ale,
  With gold of honey-jar, pinkness of hams.
      What sea-gray faces now — Balticmen? Danes?
      The table strewn with strange-carved coins.
  A dark boy asks, with voluptuous palms
   (Making shapes) about girls.

2
The Fight Between Sven and Pedro in William Clark's Ale House: 1599

Fierce music of two mouths
(Hamnavoe, winter) twixt barrel and candles.
Sven: 'Rat in the hold! Dry-rot!'
Pedro: 'Ice man!'
A Spanish sailor. A Swede.
William Clark: 'Mareon, wine to that table.'
An arm aureoled with light.
A dark hand, otter quick.
William: 'Now, gentlemen, I beg . . . .'
Concerning the fist of Sven,
It described a wide fruitless arc.
Concerning the Spanish table,
It held pots of various capacity
Before the bright rush of music, pewter to stone.
William: 'Mareon, the truncheon, quick!'
The hand of Pedro flashed twice,
A piece of sunlight fell from the beard of Sven.
Mick (Irishman): 'They'll do bloody murder. Hooray!'
Mareon's mouth was a mute hand-plucked harp.
Foot of Sven, fist of Pedro,
Flight and flash and fall of the knife.
Mixed European music, rune with rondel.
The drawn truncheon: fulcrum: point of stillness.
William: 'I now declare this war over.'
Pedro uncoils an olive hand.
Sven thrusts out a gull-bright hand.
William: 'Mareon, two glasses rum
For storm-shook haven-fast seamen.'
Pedro has kissed the beard of Sven.
In Clark's inn, white music of concord soon.

3
Sickness

William, the skull
No mistake. I counted thrice. The brewster in
    Stenness delivered *six*, not seven barrels ale.

William, the worm and the skull
Provided for. First winter here I sent for the
    lawyer. 'You won't starve, Mareon.' Quill
    and parchment and wax. The will.

William, the shroud, the worm and the skull
The sun. (Take off that crushed root and spider!)
    Breckness wind in the face. That restores me.
    Flood in the Sound — curve and brake and splash of a gull.

William, hands crossed, the shroud, the worm and the skull
Has she blown out the lamp? set traps? locked door and till?

William, the dark one, hands crossed, the shroud, the worm
    and the skull
We all go under the hill.

William, the weeping, the dark one, hands crossed,
    the shroud, the worm and the skull.
I repent me of (heartily) world-wickedness, my
    part in such, all things done ill.

William, the burning blood, the weeping, the dark one,
    hands crossed, the shroud, the worm and the skull.
It does well.

4
In Memoriam

Four hundred years since you both
Went, sundered, into the dark,
Hearts and hearthstone cold,
    William and Mareon Clark.

Search for a stone in the kirkyard —
Nothing. Never a mark.
No-one knows where your bones lie,
    William and Mareon Clark.

Even the inn you built
To hustle about the work
Of welcome and keeping, is vanished,
    William and Mareon Clark.

Your door stood open wide
From the rising of the lark
To the pole of night, to all men,
    William and Mareon Clark.

You gathered about your fires
The crew of the wintered barque
From Lisbon, or Brest, or Boston,
    William and Mareon Clark.

Did Rome and Geneva strive
For the helm of the storm-tossed kirk
Even in this quiet haven,
    William and Mareon Clark?

Tired, you'd put out the lamp,
Cover the fire, and hark!
A scatter of hooves on the cobbles,
    William and Mareon Clark.

You did not live to see
On the steep dyked westward park
The merchants' houses rising,
    William and Mareon Clark,

Tall houses hewn from granite,
Piers on the tidal mark,
Yawl and cobble noust-gathered,
    William and Mareon Clark.

Your first eyes never saw
The boys from the crofts embark
For the Davis Straits and the whale-fling,
    William and Mareon Clark,

Nor saw them come back in August,
Sovereigns sewn in each sark,
Salt men urgent for barley,
    William and Mareon Clark.

Eighteenth-century wars,
The herring shoal and the shark
Dowered that shore with silver,
    William and Mareon Clark.

Eighteenth-century wars
Doubloon and kroner and mark,
Made later taverners rich,
    William and Mareon Clark.

Graham and Gow and Millie —
You never drew the cork
For hero, pirate, spaewife,
    William and Mareon Clark.

Nothing. You cannot hear us.
Two names, quilled and stark
On a lawyer's parchment, ghostings —
   William and Mareon Clark.

Forgive this deluge of words,
First townsfolk, wherever you ark.
I have cut you dove-marks on stone:
    WILLIAM and MAREON CLARK.

Countryman

Come soon. Break from the pure ring of silence,
A swaddled wail

You venture
With jotter and book and pencil to school

An ox man, you turn
Black pages on the hill

Whisper a vow
To the long white sweetness under blessing and bell

A full harvest,
Utterings of gold at the mill

Old yarns, old malt, beside the hearth,
A breaking of ice at the well

Be silent, story, soon.
You did not take long to tell